PoetryRing Of Marriage III

I Do Romance Vows Husband & Wife Love Forgiveness

Phyllis E. Griffin

Copyright © 2022 Phyllis E. Griffin
All Rights Reserved.
HerLife HerWrite Publishing Co. LLC
ISBN: 978-1-7373740-7-7

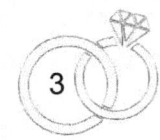

Dear Heavenly Father,

I give you glory for your inspiration and guidance in writing this book. I pray that you will use these words to bless and strengthen marriages and encourage those who desire to be married. I also pray that you use this poetry work to bring healing, hope, wisdom, and understanding in Jesus (Yeshua)'s name.
    Amen

Table of Contents

I Do	9
Marriage Is Okay	11
Have Fun	13
Make a Date	15
See the Good in Your Mate	17
Heirs of the Grace of Life Together	21
Each Voice	23
A Wife Is	25
A Wife Is Not a Maid	27
A Husband Is Not a Sugar Daddy Etc.	30
A Husband Is	32
The World & Marriage	34
Open Marriage?	36
Love Is Not a Feeling	38
Pray for Each Other	40
Be a Friend	42
Marriage Idolatry	44
Who Owns Whom?	47
Sometimes You Just Have to Say No	49
Mental Adultery	51
Emotional Adultery	55
Physical Adultery-No Touching	58
You Can't Always Get Your Way	60
Verbal Abuse	62
Mental Abuse	64
Emotional Abuse & Neglect	66
Physical Abuse-Hands to Thyself	68

Stop Threatening to Leave	70
Tried By Fire	72
Dis-Eases	75
Keep the Children Out of It	78
Watch Out for Those Dreams!	80
The Benefits of Marriage	82
In Sickness & Disease	84
Let God Get the Glory	86
Stick & Stay Together	88

I Do

I Do promise to love you until the day I die
Hear the words I say to you, for they are no lie

I Do vow to be committed to you until the end
I plan to see our relationship through thick and thin

I Do affirm that I'm not perfect, but I will do my best
I will give our relationship all I have, and on God's strength, I will rest

I Do attest that we will have some good days, some will be bad
But I will try my very best to make you comfortable and glad

I Do pledge to do my part in our relationship
I will do what I can to make it a loving, perfect partnership

I Do assure you that you are the only one in my heart
The vows I made to you, were until death do we part

I Do guarantee you that with God in my life and Jesus Christ as my Lord
I will live a life of honor toward you, by frequently taking up the holy sword

I Do give my word of honor, "I will not deliberately undermine or slight you"
I will do all that's in my power and strength, to build or edify you

I Do consent to answer any questions, you might have about me

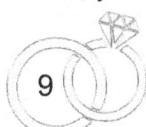

For my heart's desire is to walk in devoted love, and divine peace with thee

I Do solemnly declare, "I will keep God first in my life, only to him will you be second"
My heart will continue to be with you, and to you my hands will always reach and beckon

Marriage Is Okay

I know the world doesn't have a good opinion of marriage today
But according to the word of God, it is still a valid and beautiful way

It's a beautiful way to live your life, if you so choose
This life can add length of days to you, if you don't abuse

If you don't abuse your spouse or the privileges you are given
If you allow love and respect to be the reasons, that you are driven

To be driven by love and respect is an honorable thing
It speaks volumes to your character, and your commitment to the marital ring

The marriage ring is symbolic to a relationship that never ends
It symbolizes a union that is solidified, through thick and thin

Solidified means sticking together with some awesome, powerful glue
This glue will cause you to be united in whatever you will go through

Whatever you go through doesn't have to destroy your union
In fact, on the contrary, it can bring a more intimate communion

A more intimate communion that involves the body, soul, and spirit
A union that embarks upon a level of intimacy few relationships ever visit

Few relationships reach such a place of intimacy on this unique, committed level
Mainly because they're looking at the world or listening to the devil

Listening to the devil, will make you lose out on something that is good
It will cause you not to do your part, or do what you know you should

Do what you should do in your marriage, because marriage is okay with God
It is his idea, no matter what the world thinks! He approves of it and gives it a Nod!

Have Fun

Have fun together as husband and wife
Don't let satan keep you bowed down in ugly strife

Have fun together, take a walk and hold hands
For you are called together, she is your woman and you are her man

Have fun together, make time for a movie night
Enjoy one another's company and in each other take sure delight

Have fun together, scratch each other's back or play in each other's hair
Cherish the time you have together, be grateful God has allowed you both to be there

Have fun together, have your own playful, intimate wrestling match
Be playful and gitty because God has given you, your desirous chosen catch

Have fun together, plan to go out to eat at your favorite place
Enjoy every bite as you vastly recount, God's amazing grace

Have fun together as you plan your bright and hopeful future
Remember God is in the midst of you. Through life's challenges, he will help you maneuver

Have fun together, break out and say something that is funny
Oh…the joy it will bring while relieving stress, Bless the Lord, Honey! Honey!

Have fun together, spontaneously grab each other to do a silly step, or dance
It's things like these that can rekindle and spark a lovely, lovely romance

Have fun together, take a drive to nowhere in particular
It can open lines of communication, give opportunity to become a better listener

Have fun together, plan a day to just…be alone
These kinds of investments can yield to you a happier, more committed home

Make a Date

Make a date with your mate or spouse
A time to be together outside of the house

Make a date for just you two
A time to have intimate conversation, you with me, and I with you

Make a date to relieve all of the stress
A time to come together to straighten out any chaos or mess

Make a date together, away from the precious kids
A time to freely talk about the things, we've done or did

Make a date to go out and eat a meal
A time to laugh, be light-hearted, share what we feel

Make a date together, get away from the everyday hum-drum of life
A time to refresh and reflect on the blessings of the Lord Jesus Christ

Make a date together, get away from Everything
A time to relax and reboot, before we decide Anything

Make a date together, rekindle the fire and flames
A time to hold each other tight, relinquish all fault and blame

Make a date together, look each other in the eyes
A time to bare our hearts to one another, and expose all of satan's lies

Make a date together, whether vacation or stay-cation
A time to refresh our minds and bodies, and renew our marital motivation

Make a date together, sit quietly at the park
A time to hold hands, hear the birds sing, and deepen our marital mark

Make a date together, don't even answer a text or take a call
A time to silence all the noise around us, tear down any dividing wall

Make a date together before it's too, too late
A time to make things right with God and your precious mate

Make a date together, we have to put in the time
A time to come together now, and it doesn't have to cost a dime

Make a date together, listen to one another's heart
A time to bond and become aware of all satan's fiery darts

Make a date together, operate in God's wisdom and care
A time to foil every plot of the enemy, by showing we will make the time to be there!

See the Good in Your Mate

See the Good in Your Mate
When the husband goes into the workplace, he works to ensure the family has everything they need
He is working unto the Lord by submitting to authority and reaping financial seeds

See the Good in Your Mate
When the husband takes out the trash, preventing the home from becoming polluted
He's ensuring the atmosphere stays clean, that it remains well suited

See the Good in Your Mate
When the husband mows the lawn, he's making sure the family is safe and secure
He's ensuring snakes and rodents won't have a place to hide, so the lawn he manicures.

See the Good in Your Mate
When the husband puts gas in the car to make sure the family doesn't get stranded
He is fulfilling his role as a loving husband and father, even as, God has commanded

See the Good in Your Mate
When the husband cracks a joke that makes the wife laugh to tears
He is being used by God to bring medicine to her soul, to drive out all her fears

See the Good in Your Mate
When the husband takes the family to church, or doesn't prevent them from going
He is being loving toward his family, and respect to God, he is showing

See the Good in Your Mate
When the husband rolls up his sleeves and washes the dishes, he is showing he's willing to lighten the wife's load
He is operating in the consideration and kindness that God has truly given or bestowed

See the Good in Your Mate
When the husband sits down with the wife, listens to her problems of the day
He is showing tenderness, goodness, and love for her in a very special way

See the Good in Your Mate
When the husband agrees to watch the children, so the wife can have a time out with friends
He is acting as a selfless, caring protector, for her soul he does watch over and defend

See the Good in Your Mate
When the wife goes into the workplace, she acts as a financial helper to her spouse
She doesn't mind rising up early to help meet the needs of her house

See the Good in Your Mate

When the wife washes the dishes, she is making sure everything is nice and clean
She is working diligently to ensure a healthy environment, whether by hand or by machine

See the Good in Your Mate
When the wife cooks a meal for the family, she is ensuring they have the nourishment and strength they need
She actively works to ensure they have the nutrition and health they need to succeed!

See the Good in Your Mate
When the wife takes care of the family's clothes, she is showing her care for each member of the household
She graciously and diligently takes care of each item of clothing, hand fold by hand fold

See the Good in Your Mate
When the wife helps the children with homework, she is promoting learning, self-value, and self-esteem
She is indeed sowing seeds of patience that will help them one day realize their dreams

See the Good in Your Mate
When the wife takes the time to listen to her husband's issues or challenges, she is showing both tenderness and attentiveness
She is conveying to him respect also her desire for the relationship to continue to move in progressiveness

See the Good in Your Mate
When the wife draws a nice, hot bath for the husband, she is preparing him to be able to chill and relax
She is demonstrating her love, care, and concern for him, and Honey, that's a fact

Heirs of the Grace of Life Together

The husband and wife are heirs of the grace of life together
God has anointed them to walk together, no matter what the weather

They have been given this grace by the power or anointing of Christ
He has enabled them to walk united, through their course of life

When grace is needed, it will be dispensed
Even through life's challenges, that makes no sense

Grace is power and it is also unmerited favor
It will arrive on the scene when needed, from the blessed Savior

They are heirs or inheritors of this special, special blessing
It will bring them through whenever the enemy starts messing

They are heirs together, they are true appointed recipients
God shows up! He shows out! Because He is Omniscient

Even with grace, it doesn't mean there won't be any challenges
But the good news is, Grace will be there to help keep their balances

Being called heirs, means God sees them as equals
He doesn't slight one for the other, He deems them coequals

God has given this grace of life to them both
Because he has witnessed their commitment and heard their oath

He will not abandon them when things get difficult or hard
He will have his warring, fighting angels on post and on guard

Grace means, God will help them through it, whatever it may be
For He is watching over them, and will stop or foil every move of the enemy

Being aware of this grace, should make them hold each other tight
It should also help them squash every disagreement, before they go to bed at night

When they have a problem, grace will be there
It will give them the wisdom or skills to solve or bear

When they have difficulties, grace will arrive on the scene
It will help them maneuver through it, give them wisdom that is keen

When they feel they can't go on, grace won't let them quit,
 It will be present and give them God's strength, so that they don't relent

When they feel they need a second wind, grace will be their air
 It will pick them up above the storms of life as proof of God's divine care

Each Voice

Each voice in a marriage needs to be heard
Both are important, neither should be unobserved

When the husband speaks, the wife should listen
When the wife speaks, the husband should pay attention

Neither should say, "No, you listen to me!"
This shouldn't happen, even when or if you disagree

The voice of the wife should not overshadow the husband
She should respect his headship, shouldn't deliberately withstand

The voice of the husband should not dominate the wife
He should respect the sanctity of her rights and her life

Each spouse has a right to be heard and to be respected
This should be a mutual understanding, should be expected

Each spouse should have the freedom to give their input
This helps to develop a relationship that's hard to be shook

Each voice is needed and each is valuable
God gave each of you the ability to speak, this should be acceptable

Each spouse has the right to their own opinion
Accepting this, shows respect, and not dogmatic dominion

The husband's voice can be used to give guidance and instruction

This instruction can steer the relationship away from fatal, costly destruction

The wife's voice can be used to bring wisdom and peace
This peace can drive out confusion, and produce a relationship whose faith is concrete

Neither should say, "My voice is greater than yours, and yours is not needed."
Such a way of thinking or speaking, demonstrates a person that's indeed conceited

Each spouse should be willing to listen to the voice of one another
This mutual respect demonstrates a willingness to defer to each other

In marriage, each voice must be heard, be respected, and be valued
This makes for a healthy relationship that can gracefully be continued

A Wife Is

A wife is her husband's helper
Her job is to respect her husband, make his life better

A wife is her husband's assistant
Her job is to aid him by ensuring everything is sufficient

A wife is her husband's intimate friend
Her job is to be devoted to him until the end

A wife is her husband's personal confidant
Her job is to hold his secrets in confidence, and ensure he has no want

A wife is her husband's prayer warrior or intercessor
Her job is to pray in his behalf to the heavenly Creator

A wife is her husband's committed life partner
Her job is to cooperate, first by putting on the full armor

A wife is her husband's co-administrator
Her job is to guide the affairs of the home, be an effective collaborator

A wife is her husband's financier
Her job is to properly manage the finances and to God's law adhere

A wife is her husband's good thing and favor
Her job is to live a life of grace while submitting to the Savior

A wife is her husband's blessing from the Lord
Her job is be honorable while endeavoring to be on one accord

A wife is her husband's crown, she brings value to his life
Her job is to do well in her duties as a wife unto the Lord Jesus Christ

A wife is her husband's glory, she brings honor to his name
Her job is to walk in submission and cooperation with him, adding no shame

A Wife Is Not a Maid

A wife is not a Maid
She should be treated with respect
Daily she ministers to her family without complaining or getting upset

A wife is not a Maid
She should be treated like a precious jewel
Daily she takes care of her household, using love as her rule

A wife is not a Maid
She should be treated like a delicate flower
Daily she takes care of her family no matter what day or hour

A wife is not a Maid
She should be treated like a heavenly gift
Daily she answers the call of her household, no matter what job or shift

A wife is not a Maid
She should be treated like a queen
Daily she handles her business including making sure her house is clean

A wife is not a Maid
She should be treated as one having many degrees
Daily her family is kept and protected by her faith-filled, godly decrees

A wife is not a Maid
She should be treated like an important dignitary
Daily she rises early to ensure her family has all the things that are necessary

A wife is not a Maid
She should be treated as one having great favor with the Almighty God
Daily she guides her affairs with confidence in God's staff and rod

A wife is not a Maid
She should be treated as a great prayer warrior, one that God will hear
Daily she steps out in faith meeting life's challenges without having any fear

A wife is not a Maid
She should be treated as one having great wisdom and strength
Daily she takes care of the needs of her family, whether the first hour or the tenth

A wife is not a Maid
So please pick your clothes up off of the floor
Isn't that your responsibility, not her duty or chore?

A wife is not a Maid
So please don't deliberately make a big, huge mess
Shouldn't you be setting an example, which lessens her stress?

A wife is not a Maid
So please don't tinkle and leave it on the toilet seat

Shouldn't you out of courtesy leave it dry, clean, and neat?

A wife is not a Maid
So please don't snap your fingers to get her attention
Can't you use another way which would avoid offensive or upsetting tensions?

A wife is not a Maid
So please don't reduce her to being a slave
Walk in respect and consideration, Isn't that demonstrating the love that Christ gave?

A Husband is Not a Sugar Daddy Etc.

A husband is not a Sugar Daddy
He's not obligated to get everything the wife wants, but the things she needs
So please stop complaining and sowing those ungrateful, hateful seeds

A husband is not a Child
He's created in God's glory, should be treated like a man
So please don't handle him like one of the children, let the glory in him stand

A husband is not a little boy to be led by the wife
He has the responsibility to be the spiritual guide
So please allow him to lead and prayerfully take the ride

A husband is not some Bomb off the street
He's working with his hands, ensuring you all have somewhere to stay
So please don't speak to him disrespectfully, be careful what you say

A husband is not a Handyman
He may have some gifts or skills but may not master them all
So please don't deflate his ego, this may probably make him fall

A husband is not a Mind Reader
He doesn't always know what the wife thinks or feels
So please don't expect him to know, if you have not shared or revealed

A husband is not Omniscient or All Knowing
He doesn't know the wife's every thought or dream
So please don't exalt him to God status, and think it's okay to be mean

A husband is not an Errand Boy or Flunky
He doesn't have to do everything or go everywhere he is asked
So please don't get upset if his leadership role interferes with your 'honey do' tasks

A husband is not a 'No Matter What Wife-Pleaser'
He doesn't always say yes, though he wants to please
So please don't expect a 'yes' every time, even though he wants to applease

A husband is not a Play Toy
He shouldn't be expected to be played with or strung along
So please don't play a deceitful game with him, cause that's very, very wrong

A husband is not the Object of the Wife's Demands
He doesn't have to do everything she wants
So please don't get it twisted, or make him the subject of your insulting taunts

A husband is not a God
He doesn't have all the answers or all the solutions
So please don't look for him to solve Everything, without GOD's contributions

A Husband Is

A husband is his wife's earthly protector
His job is to shield her from harm and all predators

A husband is his wife's spiritual leader
His job is to guide her by being a holy word reader and seeder

A husband is his wife's appointed provider
His job is to minister to her needs and not to deny her

A husband is his wife's intimate confidant
His job is to hear her heart, and hold her secrets in confidence

A husband is his wife's emotional supporter
His job is to help establish her peace, help keep her emotions in order

A husband is his wife's dearest, closest friend
His job is to be committed to her through thick and thin

A husband is his wife's spiritual guide and covering
His job is to pray over her for the Holy Spirit's continual hovering

A husband is his wife's priestly example
His job is to model righteousness with his god given mantle

A husband is his wife's approachable and godly advisor
His job is to share knowledge and wisdom with her, to aid her in being wiser

A husband is his wife's suitable and covenant companion
His job is to walk in sync with her, always pursuing mutual satisfaction

The World & Marriage

We live in a world that pushes marriage to the side
But it's the very thing that can help our families survive

We live in a world that says marriage is obsolete
But it's the foundation that can make our families complete

We live in a world that thinks marriage is a joke
But it's the sacred relationship that God has spoke

We live in a world that speaks of marriage as a bondage
But it's the very thing that can prevent generational wreckage

We live in a world that says marriage is an inconvenience
But it is the relationship for which the Almighty God gives credence

We live in a world that says marriages will never last
But it can challenge our character, cause such a mindset to be left in the past

We live in a world that thinks marriage is old timey
But it can preserve our hearts, keep our feet from becoming slippery and slimy

We live in a world that says marriage is not really needed
But it can stop unnecessary pain and unfaithfulness from being seeded

We live in a world that thinks and says, marriage ain't really all this or that

But it can be the very thing that halts infightings, mutiny, and family combat

We live in a world that says marriage is just a piece of paper
But it can be the thing that gives each generation a solid anchor

We live in a world that says marriage is costly, but living together is cheaper
But it is the thing that can prove if a relationship is shallow or indeed deeper

Open Marriage?

Who in the world came up with the concept of 'an open marriage?'
This is absurd and stems from the mindset that 'marriage is bondage'

This idea definitely didn't come from The Almighty God
Heaven would declare, "This is not right but is wicked and odd"

This is indeed 'man at it again,' trying to do their own thing
Taking the sacredness out of marriage and off the marital ring

Adding more people to the holy, sacred marital relationship
Saying its okay! Because we have our own understanding and partnership!

Not being satisfied with what God has ordained
Man changed the dynamics, brought great disdain

Engaging in sex outside of marriage, polluting the union
Proud of it! Proud of it! No humility in what they're doing

People in and out of the relationship, showing no shame
Minds have been twisted by playing these dangerous games

Deceiving yourself by thinking that you're in control
Not even realizing, you're playing a simple fool's role

What will you tell your children when they are confused?
Will you tell them you're special and get to change the rules?

If you didn't want to be married, why did you say, "I DO"

Now you want to play sexual mind games, what's the matter with you?

Those who are thinking about marriage, but you're not sure
Hold off! Hold off! Until you get your heart honest and pure

"Wake up!" I say. "Wake up!" Before it's everlasting too late
Because broad is the way that leads to hell's flaming gates

But narrow is the way that leads to everlasting life
Please humble yourself under the Lordship of Jesus Christ!

Love Is Not a Feeling

Love is Not feeling, It is a commitment
One you can fulfill with God as your helper and witness

Love is Not a feeling, It is a holy promise
One you can keep if you choose to be honest

Love is Not a feeling, It is a solemn vow
One you can honor if God's word, you do allow

Love is Not a feeling, It is a lifestyle
One you can live, though you may not always smile

Love is Not a feeling, It is a God given law
One you can obey by God's presence, if you do closely draw

Love is Not a feeling, It is a heartfelt agreement
One you can respect when there's fair and equal treatment

Love is Not a feeling, It is a personal and individual decision
One you can stick with because your life is under godly submission

Love is Not a feeling, It is a personal choice
One you can execute by using your faith and lifting your voice

Love is Not a feeling, It is a sacred oath
One you can carry out as you die to selfishness, and think about you both

Love is Not a feeling, It is a godly command

One you can fulfill, when you let God be God over the woman and man!

Pray For Each Other

Pray for the person God has given to you
This is your reasonable service, the thing He wants you to do

You are both heirs of the grace of life together
Pray, Pray, Pray, that you both make it on Earth and into Heaven

Talk to God about the things you want to see in your mate
God is a transformer, so pray now, for it is not too late

Talk to Him about the things that make you mad or sad
For it is his desire to make you happy and glad

Pray in positive faith having hopeful expectations
God will hear and confirm your faith-filled declarations!

Praying means you are talking to God on behalf of your beloved
Praying means you are inviting God to intervene and manifest his divine love

Praying means you are communicating with the one that made both of you
Praying means you are speaking to the Almighty God who will show you just what to do

Pray in behalf of your spouse that God will bring about needed change
Pray for him or her that their behavior, perspective, or mindset, God will rearrange

Pray for your mate and absolutely never against him or her
This positive type of prayer God accepts. It is the only one He prefers!

Don't pray against your mate, it's like talking to the hand
Remember God is the divine creator of both the woman and the man

That's not to say you can't state your concern or even your complaint
Just know God will do things his own way, because He is God and we ain't

Pray for one another with a humble and sincere heart
He will give peace, strength, and wisdom. Yes, every attribute, He will impart

Pray, pray, pray for the one to whom you said, "I Do"
God will surely hear you and work out the union between you two

Cover your mate with prayer in their weaknesses and faults
Pray to the Father if at any time, you develop a complaint or aught

Pray for one another, it's the right thing to do
Prayer gives God the opportunity to show his everlasting love to you

Be a Friend

Be a friend to your mate before you make your vows
Spend time with each other, discover what is allowed

Be a friend to your mate after the magical words, 'I Do'
Be caring and approachable, even when you're going through

Be a friend to your mate when it's difficult to talk
Grab hands and take an long, long, intimate walk

Be a friend to your mate when they're emotionally wounded
Take time with them, don't allow or make them feel excluded

Be a friend to your mate, get to know them well
Let your knowledge of them help the relationship excel

Be a friend to your mate as you bond and grow together
Let the necessary changes happen, for they will bring you both pleasure

Be a friend to your mate, show warm mutual affection
Go the extra mile to ensure an enduring and loving connection

Be a friend to your mate, become a good, good listener
Give ear to their voice and concerns, as a caring, devoted partner

Be a friend to your mate, be honest and speak the truth
Always keep communication open, keep them in the loop

Be a friend to your mate, friends are there in the good times and the bad
Commitment and unshakeable loyalty will bring you back to the times when you were glad

Be a friend to your mate, help them challenge all of their fears
Be ready and willing to uphold them, and wipe away all of their tears

Marriage Idolatry

We can make a god out of anything, anything at all
And, as sure as we do, we are subject to fall

Make a god out of this, a god out of that
A god out of marriage, might make the Living God upset

Some people are in love with the idea of marriage, not marriage itself
They use it as a bragging right, a means to get status or respect

Some people are just in love with the idea alone…
They don't have the slightest desire to make a happy, godly home

Marriage is a calling that some are called to walk
Be careful how you handle it, Careful how you talk

Please don't get haughty, arrogant, or mean
Push the fact that you're married in someone's face, trying to be seen

Don't get on your high horse, thinking yours can't crumble
Remember you have an adversary, who would love to see you stumble

Don't put others down because they've been married more than once
Because you don't know what's going to happen in the upcoming months

Don't get prideful because you've been married to one person for many years
Because life has way of changing, it may just leave you with a bucket of tears

Don't you dare say to someone, "Na..Na..Na," to mock their singleness
You might just find Yourself lonely, and in a state of abandonment yourself

Be careful not to flaunt the fact that you're married, in order to make someone else feel bad
Because the narrative might flip one day, leaving you embarrassed and sad, sad, sad

Marriage is a calling, some are successful and unfortunately some are not
Just because yours is working now, don't forget satan always has a plot

Everyone is not called to be married and that is okay
Just live your life for God each and every day

Don't get caught up in sexual inappropriateness or sin
Let God be your companion, day by day, until the end

He will never fail you, He will forever be true
Remember, he's the one that made you, He really loves you

If you have a spouse, you should love them to the moon
But please don't put them above God, who is coming for you soon

Don't do anything for your spouse that breaks God's holy plans
Remember he is your Creator, not a woman or a man

If you disobey God for your spouse, you are making them your (god) idol
God will not be pleased! Because He alone deserves that place and title

So…don't make a god out of marriage nor your spouse
Remember God is a jealous God. He is God over Everything, without a doubt!

Be thankful for your spouse and marriage, give God all the praise!
He is to be exalted in your relationship, until the end of days

If you do this, which means you are making the decision to keep God first
He will continue to bless your union and fulfill all of your godly desires or thirsts!

Who Owns Whom?

Your spouse doesn't own you, you still belong to God
This kind of thinking is twisted and ridiculously odd

God is your Creator, He made you for his glory
You have a right to live and declare your own story

Saying, "I Do," does not mean ownership
It's agreeing to live married in equal partnership

He doesn't own you and you don't own him
You should live in agreement and treat each other like a precious gem

You have a part in the relationship and so does he
God is the one who stands in the midst of thee

Each of you have the right to think for yourself, and that's no lie
You need to respect that god given gift and not to deny

You both have been given stewardship for one another
You should have each other's back, take care of each other

No! A marriage license does not denote ownership
It is a document that solidifies a marital relationship

It is a legal document administered and given on earth
That validates a commitment and relationship's worth

It is also a document that is respected or honored in heaven

As you stood and declared your commitment, before more or less than seven

Please don't treat your spouse like a piece of your property
Treat them with respect, honor, and deserved godly dignity

Please don't tell your spouse, "You better listen to me and do what I say"
That's not the way it supposed to be, demanding in such a way

Please don't ever say to your spouse, "I own you"
They may think you're crazy, and make an appointment for you

NO to Ownership! NO to Ownership! this kind of thinking Must Go
Because relationship, partnership, and stewardship Is… the Heavenly flow

Sometimes You Just Have to Say No

Sometimes you just have to say **No** to the husband or to the wife
Saying **No** shouldn't kindle or stir up bitter, hateful strife

Say **No** to an extra financial burden, you just cannot afford
You both need to look at the situation, get on one accord

Say **No** to anything that violates your God given conscience
This will safeguard your spirit, as you walk in godly caution

Say **No** to a sexual desire that crosses biblical lines
Got to know what God expects or accepts, Don't want to walk as one blind

Say **No** to angry words, spilled out through emotional frustration
This will help establish clear boundaries in every conversation

Say **No** to someone borrowing money, you know will not pay it back
This will close the door on users, keep the family running in the black

Say **No** to charging up credit cards, so you can maintain financial stability
This will keep the family sound financially, abounding in financial security

Say **No** to an extravagant, costly vacation, that will put you in the hole
Instead, plan something locally which will help maintain your financial goals

Saying **No** to a second job, that keeps you gone or away from home
Instead, spend time developing your relationship, thereby quenching the desire to roam

Say **No** to someone coming to live in your house, who may not respect you both
This will help keep down confusion, help you keep your sacred oath

Say **No** to a pretending friend, who tries to draw you away
This will solidify your marital relationship, keep you from going astray

Say **No** to even the notion of a physical confrontation or altercation
This establishes the rules of engagement which should only involve nonviolent cooperation

Say **No** to arguing and bickering which tears down the inner soul
Instead, say yes to building each other up which is more valuable than gold

Sometimes you just have to say **No,** and that is truly a fact
Saying **No**, though it may seem negative to some, might well leave a positive, lasting impact!

Mental Adultery

Mental adultery has to do with the mind
The place where satan plays his games and seeks to undermine

He seeks to undermine anything and everything that is pure
He seeks to work on your mind and to make you unsure

Make you unsure about your marriage and about your mate
Take charge! Take charge of your mind before it's too late!

Mental adultery has to do with ideas and thoughts produced by thinking
It's your responsibility to make sure your thoughts aren't wavering or stinking

Stinking with pictures or images of someone of the past, or someone other than your spouse
Thoughts that condemn your conscience leave you feeling like a dirty louse

Thoughts about him or her that you know aren't right, but keep crossing your mind
Such thoughts you must reject and resist, and frankly you must decline

When you have thoughts like these, you have to take control
Take control before they ruin your marriage and condemn your mortal soul

These kinds of thoughts can be controlled by the words that you speak
Speak to them! Speak to them! Because you are strong and not weak

They can also be defeated by the power of Jesus (Yeshua)'s blood
Declare it! Declare it! Because you are his Beloved

The seed of mental adultery can be planted in dreams
You see our adversary, the devil, doesn't care how he lies or schemes

He will give you a dream about someone of the past, or someone you work with
All he wants is to destroy your marriage or cause an unnecessary, painful rift

He will try to seduce you in the middle of your god given sleep
This reveals his slimy character because he is really just a creep

He will also cause some beautiful or handsome person to cross your path
Catch your eyes to fill them with lust, but before you act, you better do the math!

Take control of your eyes, don't let your looking turn into lust
For if you look too… long, your marital relationship just might go bust

Remember you're not a little boy or girl that can afford to play flirty games

Realize the enemy plays for keeps, he'll bring you down to humiliating shame

Also, remember the bible says, if you look at a person to lust after them
You have already committed adultery. Therefore, it is imperative that you avoid being condemned!

You can't stop adulterous thoughts or images from coming, because they surely will
But you can stop them from manifesting, by your words and the blood which prevents their ungodly steal

Speak up! Speak up! And say this, the moment that you awake
"Get behind me satan, for my marriage and my family you will Not surely take!"

"I declare this weapon of adultery that you have formed against me, shall not prosper
In the name of Jesus and by the power of his blood, I will Not give in to this sinful pressure"

The enemy uses mental adultery to seduce, entice, and make you think 'the grass is greener on the other side'
But please be aware of his seductions because his objective is for your feet to be on a slippery slide

Mental adultery can become a stronghold (mindset) in the human mind
Bombarding you with seducing thoughts and images to make or force you to resign

Resign to a false truth or illusion, so that to seduction and enticement you do yield
Reduce you to becoming just another person or statistic of one playing the field

But don't you believe the lie, not even for a moment
Remember God is about truth, He is the Great Marriage Proponent

So if you have thoughts of adultery, please don't feel or be condemned
Just know assuredly they are not coming from God, but are coming from him

The very one that comes to steal, kill, and destroy
The very one that comes to strip you of your marriage, focus, and your joy

Emotional Adultery

Emotional adultery has to do with emotions, passions, and feelings
The enemy catches us when we're vulnerable, when our life is reeling

When you have a desire or need to be heard or held
You have to be careful that the desire or need doesn't lead to the bed

The enemy says, "You can talk to him or her so easy about everything
because your spouse won't listen to you, no not about anything"

The enemy perpetrates and pushes this lie to get you ensnared
Not that he is concerned about your issue, because he never cared

But because he wants to ruin your marriage, cause you to fail
All because he wants you to miss heaven and fall into hell

So…getting our emotions tied or connected to someone else
Could prove devastating or dangerous, even cause us to welch

Getting emotionally tied to someone of the opposite sex
Could breed more problems, make our life more complex

Yes, you may have some things in common, see some things the same
But be careful to draw the line, so the relationship doesn't end in shame

Having an emotional connection with someone is all well and good

But if it crosses the line, take heed! Do what you know you should

You may think or say, "he or she is so… willing to listen to me"
But maybe the truth is, he or she is desiring something more… of thee

You may think 'he or she is really willing to spend time with me'
But perhaps, you need to rethink their motives, one might agree

Be careful thinking 'you have to talk to a particular person' when facing difficulties
This might be a red flag which says, you're too dependent on them for your security

Be careful not to allow friendship with the opposite sex to alienate your affection
from the one you're committed to
Be alert! Be aware! Because sometimes this is what the enemy really wants to do

Always consider your spouse first when you have emotional needs
Let them be the first one to minister to you, and plant some healing seeds

Secondly, when you need that tenderness to sooth your deep, deep emotions
Run to God, allow his spirit and his word to be your heavenly portion

His word will give you peace when you are going through emotional whims

He will give you stability and strength, show you that your answer is in Him!

Physical Adultery-No Touching

Physical adultery is when a husband or wife has sex with someone outside the marital union
This choice or decision could lead to bitterness, strife, or a fatal collusion

It is a decision that is rooted and grounded in pride
It is never acceptable to have an affair or relationship on the side

This decision is not right, in fact, it's very, very wrong
Somebody's got to answer to God that sits on the throne

It is a decision that is embedded in huge ego and pure selfishness
It is committed out of a lack of wisdom and frankly foolishness

Satan comes to entice and suggest that 'the grass is greener on the other side'
But he fails to mention, if we participant in this act, God's word we have defied

Physical adultery can lead to the breaking up of the home
The offended spouse then has the right to say, "I'm definitely gone!"

This choice or decision can lead to sickness or sexually transmitted disease
Beloved, this goes to show us that we can't do whatever we please

Physical adultery can also lead to marital divorce
On the other hand, sexual faithfulness can keep us out of the courts

This decision can end in the very loss of life
Because it plays to the spirits of jealousy, murder, and contentious strife

Physical adultery is not the will or expectation of God, our Creator
Therefore, He will deal with the matter and with every hater or frustrator

Outside the marriage there shouldn't be any touching, kissing, or sex talk
Be bold and courageous! tell the devil he's got to walk!

Oh, do you think you can put hot coals in your bosom and not be burned?
There are many that have fallen before you, because this lesson they didn't learn

Now, it is always God's desire to protect us from the enemy or our adversary
But we must cooperate with Him, do the things that we know are necessary

We must close every door and sometimes don't even answer the phone
This can be a sure-fire message to the hunter, that he or she, Better Gone!

The bibles tells us to flee from fornication and all sexual sins
If we choose to do this, our marriage can triumph and win!

You Can't Always Get Your Way

You can't always get your way in marriage,
Remember it's no longer all about you
May I please remind you of the words you said,
they were, "I Do."

You can't walk in selfishness,
Ranting and raving about what you want
Showing out and getting loud!
All in public or up in a restaurant.

You've got to see the bigger picture now,
Because it's not one but two
I know it's difficult for you,
But it's time to grow up, Boo.

Putting yourself first always
is a thing of the past
You see the is the only way
This relationship is going to last.

All this attitude of
"I'm going to get my way,"
Will definitely leave you as a loner
Cause your hair to turn gray and gray.

You make yourself an idol,
Put yourself on a throne
You exalt your self-importance
But this my Dear, is wrong, wrong, wrong.

That's not to say that you're not important
Because you know that you are
But should your pride and arrogance
Make one feel like a prisoner behind bars?

If you have to have your way in Everything
You're going to have some…trouble
Please know you're not living in reality
cause no one is going to agree with 'Everything in your bubble!'

You push and push, nag and nag
Until your spouse gives in
Again, you're showing your ugly pride
Which is a selfish, hateful sin

You may say, "It's my way or the highway"
but you might well be careful what you say
Because this might prove to be the wrong time to push and demand
because your spouse may indeed go away, and this time to stay!

Humble yourself under the mighty hand of God, our Father
Give in to your spouse from time to time
Let them have the lead or have their way
This takes nothing away from you, and is certainly not a crime.

Learn to walk away from the mindset of selfishness
Consider your spouse in everything you do
Live a life of spousal inclusion and consideration
This will crucify the selfish '*I or Me*' in you, in everything you both pursue.

Verbal Abuse

Verbal abuse has to do with words and how they are used
Unfortunately, some choose to use their words to hurt and abuse

Using words to demean or belittle someone is never acceptable
Words have power and dominion, are not so easily retractable

Calling someone out of their god given name
Is painful and disrespectful, causes tremendous pain

Cursing at or cussing at someone because you think you have the right
Is not showing love at all, it is a spirit of bitter, hateful spite

Screaming or yelling at someone to gain or maintain control
Is a form of verbal abuse, disturbs both the spirit and the soul

Using words to make or force someone to coward down to you
Is manipulation, control, and frankly, verbal abuse too

Again, verbal abuse has to do with words that are strongly spoken
Words that are harsh, cruel, and mean, void of any joking

This kind of abuse can break your heart
It can set a husband and wife definitely apart

Verbal abuse is spitting out or blurting out words, like you just don't care
It is abuse that no one should experience, go through, or even have to share

Verbal abuse is like sending a dagger into someone's innermost being
It is abuse that damages a person, in a way that people aren't seeing

Verbal abuse is like hitting someone with deliberate, crushing blows
Hard to accept from a spouse, but yes, from your enemies or foes

Verbal abuse is when a spouse uses words to reduce their partner to a child
Using demeaning and belittling words, in order to control and beguile

Verbal abuse is speaking horrible words or calling a spouse out of their name
Using ugly and vulgar words, in order to keep someone in bondage and chains

Verbal abuse is always pointing out someone else's flaws and faults
It's constantly hounding someone about their wrong, and in their wounds skillfully pouring salt

Verbal abuse should not be accepted nor tolerated, it should not be allowed
It should be dealt with openly, honestly, and sincerely, so that it is effectively disallowed

Verbal abusers can be delivered, in fact, they can be changed
If they make the decision, and allow their hearts, minds, and language to be rearranged

Mental Abuse

Mental abuse is closely related to verbal abuse, it involves the use of words
Manipulative words that are spoken, like the despicable droppings of birds

Words that are used to twist your self-image, reduce, and bring you to nought
Such words' mission are to reframe your thinking, so you don't think of yourself, as you ought

Mental abusers will emphasize your weight and tell you, "No one else will love or want you"
Their goal is to make you feel trapped and helpless, to ensure you stick to them (abuser) like glue

Mental abusers will always find a way to put you down, make you feel like trash
They will take your self-esteem and self-worth, and slowly reduce it to mash

Mental abusers like verbal abusers are bullies, they love to start or pick fights
They have little regard for peace or respect, they frequently trample on others' rights

Humiliation is a part of mental abuse, the piercing or subtle insults that are said
They are used to bring submission or control, by dominating the thoughts in your head

False accusation is also a part of mental abuse, where a spouse is frequently accused of something
No matter how they try to explain or convince their spouse otherwise, they're left on the hook for most anything

Blame is another component of mental abuse, Blaming, Blaming, Blaming!
One spouse refuses to take responsibility for their actions, so they shift to spousal Shaming!

In the case of blaming, comments like "It's your fault and it happened because of you!" are commonly used
These are the words used to escape accountability or responsibility, by the one that has abused

Verbal assaults or insults are common with mental abuse, sometimes brazen and sometimes subtle
They are used to control and bow the will of its subject, leaving them in a victimized state of rubble

Emotional Abuse & Neglect

Emotional abuse has to do with the abuse of feelings or emotions which encroaches on a person
It is abuse that toys with one's emotions, causing them to range from stability to levels that worsen

An emotional abuser will dismiss your feelings or even your right to feel
They will mock your expressed feelings, try to convince you, they're not real

The emotional abuser will demand the suppression of your feelings, tell you they're just in your head
But you must stand for your individuality, deal with your feelings, realize you can't bury them as though they were dead

Emotional abuse also has to do with abandonment, leaving someone alone to suffer
Such suffering in silence is cruel and selfish, so is being left to drown in your sorrow with no one or nothing to be your buffer

This kind of abuse though not physical can reach deep into the soul and spirit of man
It can cause unchangeable, piercing damage, can twist or distort God's will or plan

An emotional abuser demonstrates no empathy, has little or no heart
These kinds of responses or lack thereof, will drive the couple apart

Rejection commonly shows up in an emotional abusive situation

Rejecting one's opinion, thoughts, or ideas to inflict further frustration

The emotional abuser is one that utters or spits out threats upon threats
Threatening to leave, put the spouse out, to become physical, having no remorse or regrets

Emotional abuse also comes with taunting, jeering, and of course, name calling
The abuser feels big when using 'put downs' or 'verbal criticism,' which is quite appalling

This abuse has a damaging effect on one's self-esteem and socialization
It oppresses one's self-worth or self-confidence through different forms of humiliation

An emotional abuser is a 'bully' that has never addressed their own fears or pain
Therefore, they seek to control others, rather than deal with their own fears, pain, insecurities, or shame

Please remember that God has not created you to be the victim of anyone's abusive behavior
For, He is your God and Creator, and his son is your Lord and Savior!

Physical Abuse-Hands to Thyself

Physical abuse is never, ever okay
This must be understood the very first day

Not a slap in the face or push against the wall
This is not acceptable, no not at all

No punching! No punching! Keep your hands to yourself
This kind of thing can lead to someone's death

Feet are made for walking and certainly not for kicking a spouse
What in the world is wrong with you, you cowardly mouse?

Hands around the throat, trying to choke each other out
Fighting like cats and dogs, kids crying and screaming all about

Hitting with the fist or with an open hand
Stop this! Stop this! Oh, foolish woman and man

You may think you can do this, just because you can
But remember, before the judgment seat you will surely stand

Hitting with an object, getting a mop or broom
All because you've neglected to give the Almighty room

Using your feet to stomp your spouse in the most private place
Pray now! Because you're definitely going to need the power of God's grace

Black and blue bruises on the face, arms, and the chest

You better know assuredly, this is not acceptable! This is some unholy mess!

A mess that God will surely get in the midst of
Cry out to him, oh woman or man, for he still lives up above

Causing bruises, breaking bones, or the giving of a black eye
Then you cry and say, "I'm sorry," confess your Love, Now you know that's a Lie

Abusing each other, causing swelling in the body which is God's temple
Awake! Oh foolish man or woman. Stop being brutish and simple

Physical abuse from a man or woman is never, never alright
Spouses should be treated with dignity and respect in the living God's sight

Experiencing physical abuse is Not a part of the suffering of Christ
Please seek to get out of the situation while it's day. Don't wait until it is night

Physical abuse means someone has unresolved issues and pain
But don't you be their punching bag, don't let them drive you insane!

You have a right to be treated with respect and that doesn't mean laying on of hands
Find a safe way to make your exit, and with wisdom and strength, Do take your stand!

Stop Threatening to Leave

Stop threatening to leave every time there is a spat
It's time to grow up now, you need to realize that

Stop threatening to leave every time you don't get your way
You need to realize that that's not reality, realize it today!

Stop threatening to leave every time you don't get everything you want
Your selfish and rash decisions may one day come back to haunt

Stop threatening to leave every time you get angry or mad
You decide today, whether you will be happy or sad

Stop threatening to leave every time you're displeased
Learn to humble yourself, get down on your bending knees

Stop threatening to leave every time you don't get a sexual thrill
Remember, every encounter is not the same, you got to be real

Stop threatening to leave every time someone tries to flirt with your mate
The devil, our adversary, will use this as his divisive or destructive bait

Stop threatening to leave every time you have a disagreement with your in-laws
From the bible's point of view, leaving your spouse for this reason is not a just cause

Stop threatening to leave every time you don't see eye to eye
You are two people becoming one, so please don't believe or fall for satan's lie

Stop threatening to leave every time church people or family members come against you
Remember the commitment you made to each other. Stand and Be true!

Stop threatening to leave thereby invoking fear and instability in your spouse
Change your words, behavior, or responses. And, Your Threats you will be able to Denounce!

Stop threatening to leave every time things seems to go wrong
Be Proactive! Stand on the word of God! And, You Will Be Strong!

Tried By Fire

Every marriage will be tried by fire, no matter who you are
You may be the president, the first lady, or even a movie star

The fire will come to shake your foundation, to see what sort it's of
You must remember to humble yourself, call on the God above

The fire might come because the past wants to rear up its ugly head
You must realize your past Is Over! Over! Take your authority, put that dragon to bed!

The fire might come because of a sudden sickness or disease
But you must Stand! And, Believe the Almighty will bring healing and ease

The fire might come because someone has chosen to scandalize your name
But Stand Firm in the face of it, refuse to surrender to scandal or shame

The fire might come because someone has raised a false accusation against your life
But look to God who knows everything, and trust in your Lord Jesus Christ

The fire might come because a spouse gets laid off, now has no employment
Trust God in the midst of it all, He will open a new door for reemployment

The fire might come because a third party tries to invade your relationship
This is a critical time to pull together, show forth a more united partnership

The fire might come because your relatives don't like your mate or spouse
But remember you made a commitment to live with him or her in the house

The fire might come because of the death of a family member or friend
Through this time of sorrow, you both be determined to be committed until the end

The fire might come because of heavy financial burdens, you can't see your way out
God is a faithful Father, He will see you through, so just believe and do not doubt

The enemy brings or creates the fire to steal the marital relationship
But God allows the fire to purify and solidify the marital partnership

The enemy brings the fire to divide the marriage or this sacred union
But God allows the fire so he might bring forth a more united marital communion

The enemy brings the fire to destroy marriage or this holy institution
But God allows the fire in order to build a strong marital foundation

The enemy creates the fire to make mockery of God's divine marital plan
But God allows the fire so that he can show his glory between the woman and the man

So realize that No marriage is exempted from going through fiery trials or the fire
But if each couple trusts God through the process, they might get the marriage that they so desire!

Dis-Eases

In the course of married life, you will definitely encounter Dis-Eases
There will be things that are not pleasant, things that leave you displeased

But don't be discouraged, don't throw in the towel
Because you will have to fight Dis-eases, mile after mile

But if you choose to fight, you can surely win
Even if they confront you over and over again

These are some of the Dis-Eases that you will surely encounter:

The Dis-Ease of Disappointment
When things don't go your way
You have to make to the decision if you will go or stay

The Dis-Ease of Disrespect
Yes, there will be times when you or your spouse feels disrespected
Though this is not ideal or acceptable, It should be expected

The Dis-Ease of Dissatisfaction
In marriage, there will be times when one spouse doesn't feel happy or fulfilled
But be careful in such times, that to temptation you do not yield

The Dis-Ease of Disagreement
We must dispel the myth that says, married couples don't or won't have disagreements

However, those disagreements can become a safe place to bear your hearts and vent

The Dis-Ease of Discommunication
Communication is one of the most vital things in a marital relationship
If a spouse feels dissed or dismissed, this can damage or cause a breach in the partnership

The Dis-Ease of Disapproval
In every relationship, each person strives and craves to be approved of or accepted
Where there is an absence of approval, it is easy for that person to feel rejected or dejected

The Dis-Ease of Distrust
Distrust means something has happened or has been said to cause trust to be broken
Then trust can only be restored by a change of actions and assuring words that are spoken

The Dis-Ease of Disorder
Disorder denotes that things in the relationship are out of order or out of control
This means such things must be addressed, set back in order, to regain balance in the marital soul

The Dis-Ease of Dismay
Dismay means a feeling of being confounded, baffled, or confused
This feeling or emotion can manifest when negativity, rejection, or pain is infused

The Dis-Ease of Disconnection

Disconnection means the sense of belongingness or intimacy in the relationship has been breached

Connectedness can be restored when heart-to-heart communication is carried out or reached

Keep the Children Out of It

Keep the children out of the marital disagreements
Use discretion when expressing your personal Dis-easements

Keep the children out of the arguing and the fussing
Please don't stoop to the low level of vulgar yelling and cussing

Keep the children out of the adult communications or conversations
Protect their minds and hearts from preventable anguish and frustrations

Keep the children out of the heated, angry disputes
Unless, you want them to mimic you, and one day give you a rebuke

Keep the children out of your negative or critical opinions of your mate
Guard or shield their precious spirits from your bitterness and hate

Keep the children out of having to ever choose sides
Don't make them choose between you both because of your ego or pride

Keep the children out of being used as a strategy or mighty weapon
Who knows if you're not creating your own Armageddon?

Keep the children out of personal, emotional disappointments with one another
Learn to handle them like adults should, and work things out with each other

Keep the children out of money matters or your financial affairs
Handle your adult business, and address your financial needs to God in prayer

Keep the children out of adult matters, for they're too weighty for them to handle
Let them be children while they can, and you both be the responsible adult examples!

Watch Out for Those Dreams!

Dreams are pictures that come in your head
They come while you're sleeping or slumbering in bed

Dreams can show you all kinds of things
They might even convince you to give up your ring

Dreams can lie, show you or your spouse are doing wrong
They come for one purpose, to break up your home

Dreams can suggest that someone has been unfaithful
They will have you waking up, acting mean and hateful

Dreams can portray you as being disloyal
Because satan wants somebody to see a lawyer

Dreams can show pictures of you or your spouse, 'Just going off!'
Because the enemy wants to make mockery of your marriage, he loves to scoff

Dreams can seem to be so… very, very real
But don't forget the enemy comes to steal and to kill

Dreams can show you that you or your spouse are walking out
All because the enemy has sown or planted a seed of doubt

Dreams can distort or twist the truth
They are designed to start trouble, kindle disputes

Dreams can have you at odds with one another

Have you thinking, you need to go back home to your mother

Dreams can have you mad, mad, mad
They can kill your confidence and joy, make you sad, sad, sad

Dreams can sow into your heart a seed of mistrust
They can make you shut down, instead of, wanting to talk or discuss

Dreams can come after experiencing satisfying sexual intimacy
They come to falsely accuse a spouse of committing indecency or adultery

Dreams can come before you get a promotion or financial blessing
They'll have you pointing the finger at each other, Watch Out!
'Cause the enemy is messing'

The bible instructs us to tell a dream as a dream
As we keep this in mind, remember the enemy always has a plot or scheme.

It also tells us to walk in love and try the spirit by the spirit
Therefore, use God's discernment to determine if a dream has any truth or merit

This poem is not meant to say that all dreams mislead, deceive, or lie
However, before you act on a dream, do your homework! Seek God before you tell your spouse, Goodbye!

The Benefits of Marriage

There are benefits in marriage,
 no matter what the world may say
God rewards those who chooses to do things his righteous way

There is the benefit of statistically living a life that is longer
This perhaps is because of the couples' love for each other
 or their combined Faith in God may also be stronger

There is the benefit of 'two being better than one'
Where they both have a reward for their labor
One can uphold the other as they devote themselves to the wonderful Savior

There is the benefit of living a life of stableness or stability
Finally, feeling at home with the one you love
No longer a need to wander or participant in endless mobility

There is the benefit of sexual fulfillment and fidelity
Having a marriage that is satisfying and exclusive
Not looking elsewhere for satisfaction or for relationships that are elusive

There is the benefit of true companionship
Having someone that is there for you, spending quality time with you
They are there to assist you in whatever you need them to do

There is the benefit or blessing of financial prosperity
Having two people working and putting their resources together

Helps to beat down the yoke of poverty, lessens its possibility

There is the benefit of having children that are happier and stable
Children who grow up having both parents in their lives
Are perhaps more apt to be successful and make greater strides

There is the benefit of being heirs together of God's grace
God sees both of you. You are his son and she is his daughter
He supplies the grace needed to ensure you treat each other as you ought to

There is the benefit of God being your Defense
He fights for marriages because they are a part of his divine plan
He will defend the marital unit, against any organization, woman, or man

There is the benefit of immediate counsel within your own walls
You can bounce ideas and concerns off of each other
Therefore, you can be more equipped to answer life's challenges, whenever they call

There is the benefit of praying together, calling on God's name
In the midst of difficulty, you know exactly where to go
Because you're acutely aware of God's intervention, you know it can bring great change!

In Sickness & Disease

Usually at the start of marriage, both parties are healthy and strong
But we know as life happens, things can go critically wrong

One single diagnosis can change your world
One single diagnosis can make your head swirl

One bout with sickness can impact your health
It can also change your financial status or wealth

But, not matter if sickness or disease come or go
The commitment to love should continue to grow

Being there to serve each other, day by day
Showing love and compassion is the bible way

Your spouse is not the same, neither are you
But you have God's promise to walk you through

Practicing patience is more in demand
Operating in forbearance is your humble stance

Being more and more considerate, than you've ever been
Is the virtue you must demonstrate to your closest kin?

Going to appointments here and there
Being there! Being there! Showing you care!

Assisting with exercise, medication, and life skills
Resisting the enemy who wants to steal and kill

Praying for him or her for recovery and healing
Those prayers of Faith will stop the enemy from stealing

When you took the vow, you said, "I Do" in sickness and in health
Now you must keep your promise and refuse to welch

When your beloved is going through sickness or disease
Do your best in every way to bring them relief and ease

Let God Get the Glory

Let God get the glory out of you as you make the decision to marry
He will help you through every obstacle if you allow Him to carry

Carry you through all the good times and through the bad
He is a stick and stay God, who knows how to make you strong and glad

Marriage is not something you can make it through without any help
God will be there every step of the way to ensure that you are kept

So you've seen some fail at marriage, now your heart is filled with fear
But, Arise and Shine! Now look to God, for He is very near

Perhaps, you cannot model your life or marriage, after what you have seen
But if you listen to God, He can shape your marriage. Instruct you through everything

If you're willing to listen to Him, it will make the severing difference
His instructions can change your outcome, and bring mighty, mighty deliverance

What happened in someone else's marriage, should not be your measuring stick
No! Everyone makes their own choices in the time of peace and bitter conflict

The marriage walk is not easy, neither is it for the impatient or the faint
Know that you will surely need God because a piece of cake it ain't

However, if you use the ingredients of humbleness, forgiveness, and walk in godly love
You will have all the assistance of heaven to establish a marriage ordained from above

Marriage is surely hard work and sometimes you will literally have to cry
But the beauty that can be produced can cause you to have a gracious sigh

So let God get the glory out of you and your marriage, don't let others be your excuse
He will be working with you both, so a good marriage you can produce

If for some reason, you did not have a successful marriage in the past
Don't be afraid to try again! God is able to give you one that can last!

Stick & Stay Together

Stick and Stay Together
No matter what people say
Remember you will stand before God on the appointed day

Stick and Stay Together
No matter the opinions of others
Remember this relationship is not about your sister, brother, or mother

Stick and Stay Together
No matter how people come against you Both
Remember it was before God you stood and made this oath

Stick and Stay Together
No matter how many hard times you see
Remember the Almighty God is truly in the midst of thee

Stick and Stay Together
No matter if you have times of sickness and disease
Remember God will never forsake you, He will bring healing and ease

Stick and Stay Together
No matter if you experience poverty and lack
Remember God, our Heavenly Father, will be there and will take up the slack

Stick and Stay Together
No matter how people talk

Remember God has called you together, your assignment is the marital walk

Stick and Stay Together
No matter how much people don't like your mate
Remember God has given you both responsibility, your decisions will determine your fate

Stick and Stay Together
No matter how satan tries to pry you apart
Remember God expects you to live by his word that has been planted in your hearts

Stick and Stay Together
No matter your ups and downs
Remember God is well able to make your marriage happy and sound

Stick and Stay Together, Stick and Stay Together
No matter what comes or goes
Remember to Speak out to God. Call on Him. For, He is the God who knows

www.ingramcontent.com/pod-product-compliance
Lightning Source LLC
Chambersburg PA
CBHW070937160426
43193CB00011B/1721